IMAGES
of America
MONTEREY'S
HOTEL DEL MONTE

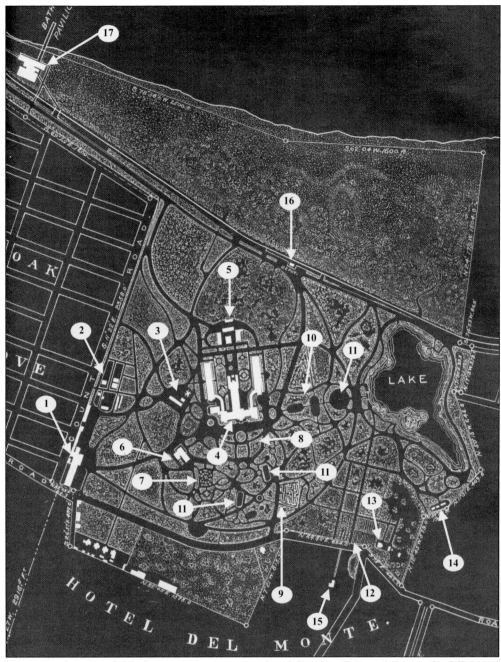

This map of the Hotel del Monte's 126-acre park is dated October 1907, and depicts the following: 1) stable, 2) nursery, 3) water tank and firehouse, 4) hotel, 5) laundry and staff housing, 6) clubhouse, 7) Arizona Garden, 8) South Gardens, 9) maze, 10) East Gardens, 11) tennis courts, 12) cutting gardens, 13) gardener's cottage, 14) Chinese quarters, 15) St. John's Chapel, 16) train depot, and 17) bathhouse. (Courtesy of Special Collections, Stanford University.)

ON THE COVER: Guests stroll through the formal South Gardens of the Hotel del Monte, justly renowned for its magnificent grounds.

IMAGES
of America
MONTEREY'S
HOTEL DEL MONTE

Julie Cain

ARCADIA
PUBLISHING

Published by Arcadia Publishing
Charleston, South Carolina

Printed in the United States of America

Library of Congress Catalog Card Number: Applied for

For all general information contact Arcadia Publishing at: 2005927547
Telephone 843-853-2070
Fax 843-853-0044
E-mail sales@arcadiapublishing.com
For customer service and orders:
Toll-Free 1-888-313-2665

Visit us on the Internet at www.arcadiapublishing.com

Mom, this one is for you.

"The hotel is first seen through a vista of trees, and in its beautiful embowerment of foliage and flowers, resembles some rich private home in the middle of a broad park . . . The gardener's art has turned many acres into a choice conservatory, where the richest flowers bloom in profusion." Artist Harry Fenn's drawing illustrates perfectly the sentiment of this quote from a Hotel del Monte pamphlet. (Courtesy of author.)

CONTENTS

Acknowledgments   6

Introduction   7

1.   First Hotel: 1880–1887   9

2.   Second Hotel: 1887–1924   55

3.   Third Hotel: 1924–1942   99

Illustration Credits   125

Bibliography   126

ACKNOWLEDGMENTS

I want to thank several people who have helped me with research and preparation for this book. Some live on the Monterey Peninsula, while others reside closer to my native turf, the San Francisco Bay Area. They have all been incredibly generous with their time, support, and enthusiasm.

First off is Pat Hathaway, owner of a large historical photographic archive (California Views) based in Monterey. He provided many hours of his time to make available and scan over 100 images for Monterey's Hotel del Monte and was unflagging in the search for just the right photograph.

Another person of great help was Dennis Copeland, archivist of the Monterey Public Library, who oversees the wonderful resources found in the California History Room, including the Julian Graham photograph collection. I'd like to thank Dennis, as well as Terry L. Anderson and Barbara Briggs-Anderson, for permission to reproduce many of the Graham photographs used in the third chapter.

At Stanford University, the Special Collections and Archives staffs worked hard to locate and photocopy hotel-related materials. Christy Smith did an excellent job scanning both the university-owned photographs and images from my own collection.

Elizabeth Byrne, head librarian of the Environmental Design Library at UC Berkeley, was very helpful with providing related copyright information. Both she and reference librarian Debby Sommer were very supportive of this project.

Marlea Graham, good friend and research partner, put in long hours and many miles driving me back and forth from the Bay Area to Monterey. She also helped with research, locating and photocopying materials, making suggestions, and proofing the text.

Mr. Elmer Lagorio, retired archivist for the Pebble Beach Company, was very generous many times in sharing with me his own research of the Hotel del Monte. I'd also like to thank Neal Hotelling, director of licensing for the Pebble Beach Company, for allowing me to come and look at images there.

John Sanders and Allyn McGuire of the Naval Postgraduate School provided me with maps of the hotel grounds that were invaluable. John also made available the images of Carl Stanley and Amelia Earhart used in this book. Pete Charette, also at the NPS, shared his extensive collection of Hotel del Monte ephemera with me.

Mona Gudgel of the Monterey County Historical Society in Salinas helped to answer some of my questions about the 1887 fire, locating the Simmons trial transcript for me.

Last, but not least, a special thank you to my neighbors (and stalwart computer supporters!) Judy Kintz and Vicky Pennewell.

INTRODUCTION

I "discovered" the Hotel del Monte while researching the historic Arizona Garden at Stanford University in 1998. Looking through an old book about the school, I came across an advertisement for the hotel. I found out that this hotel had been world famous for its beautiful grounds, which included an Arizona Garden similar to the one at Stanford. Wanting to know more about the Del Monte Arizona Garden, I looked at literally hundreds of photographs of the hotel grounds, and thus the spell was cast. I fell in love with the romance of the hotel, my imagination forever captured by the evocative images themselves.

I also learned that the Hotel del Monte was built by the Pacific Improvement Company (PIC) in 1880 to generate passenger trade for the railroad. The PIC was a holding company for the owners of the Southern Pacific Railroad Company, a group of former Sacramento merchants widely known as the "Big Four."

Charles Crocker, Collis P. Huntington, Mark Hopkins, and Leland Stanford had all invested in and built the western half of the first transcontinental railroad. Crocker took the most personal interest in the creation of the hotel. He vowed that it would rival, if not outclass, any other resort hotel in America or Europe. Built in an astounding 100 days, the Hotel del Monte would prove to be popular with the wealthy and influential members of American society for generations to come.

Several factors contributed to the hotel's success. Monterey was a perfect site to build a resort hotel, with spectacular scenery and a colorful past as California's first capital. The mild climate allowed guests to visit any time of the year, an uncommon practice for resorts of the 1880s. The hotel accommodations were first rate and included state-of-the-art rarities such as piped hot and cold water to all three floors and "telephonic communication" between the hotel and stable. The dining fare was superb, and no expense was spared on the elegant furnishings.

Not content with landscaping the 126 acres that surrounded the hotel, the PIC purchased an additional 7,000 acres (today's Del Monte Forest) to serve as a playground for the guests. They built a scenic roadway, later known as 17-Mile Drive, that began at the hotel and swept along the coastline and through the forest before winding back to the hotel's front door. Picnics were held at various rest stops along the way, including Pebble Beach. A glass-roofed swimming pavilion, a racetrack, a small lake for boating and fishing, and several lawn tennis courts also provided recreational entertainment.

The hotel burned completely to the ground on April 1, 1887. Plans to rebuild on a more elaborate scale were announced immediately; the second hotel opened eight months later. Construction of the Del Monte Golf Course in 1897 was one of the continued improvements made for guests. It is the oldest course in continuous operation west of the Mississippi, and its popularity eventually led S. F. B. Morse to develop the Pebble Beach Golf Links. Morse purchased the hotel and Del Monte Forest in 1919 and ordered construction of the third Hotel del Monte after fire struck again in 1924. This Spanish Colonial Revival–style building, as luxuriously appointed as its Victorian predecessors, was completed in 1926.

The United States government requisitioned the hotel from Morse as a pre-flight training facility in 1942. After the war, they bought the hotel and a portion of the grounds, then moved the Naval Postgraduate School there in 1952.

The hotel was California's first destination resort. Its long-term success established the Monterey Peninsula as a world-class tourist mecca. The owners promoted sports such as golf, polo, and tennis, resulting in major competitions and tournaments being held on the hotel grounds from the late 1890s onward. Hotel visitors included dignitaries, businessmen, and members of high society, as well as presidents and politicians. Rutherford B. Hayes visited the hotel in 1880, and President McKinley ran the country from the "Queen of American Watering Places" for a week in 1901. Two years later, Theodore Roosevelt galloped around 17-Mile Drive in record time. Foreign royalty frequented the hotel, as did Hollywood's elite during the 1930s.

A photographer was associated with each hotel. C. W. J. Johnson set up shop in Monterey shortly after the first hotel opened, then established a photographic parlor on the grounds in 1887. He was followed by Richard Arnold, who took hundreds of photographs of the second hotel. Julian P. Graham began working for Morse in 1924, just before the fire. These men were artists, and each left behind a legacy of work that captured a time now vanished. What follows on these pages is just a small fraction of what they saw and recorded. The images and photographs follow a rough chronology, providing crystalline memories of "the most elegant seaside establishment in the world."

This panorama of the southwestern end of the Hotel del Monte shows two buggies and an automobile parked beneath the shady oaks, while three men gaze toward the veranda. Several more automobiles directly opposite the main entrance are perhaps off to the racetrack or preparing for a jaunt along 17-Mile Drive. Either destination was a popular choice at the turn of the century. (Courtesy of Pat Hathaway.)

One

FIRST HOTEL
1880–1887

I have become thoroughly alive to the importance of doing something in Monterey.

—Charles Crocker

This extremely rare stereo view of the first hotel, still under construction, shows a group of workers on the roof directly above the front doors and another worker leaning out of an upper-story window. Railroad crews brought in by the PIC built the hotel in just 100 days, under the able direction of Superintendent Stephen Longstreet. The cost was $250,000. (Photograph by A. W. Fell; courtesy of Pat Hathaway.)

Charles Crocker was "a doer, not a talker," by his own account, and his exuberant manner of dealing with the building of the Hotel del Monte was typical of his dynamic personality. He is seated (center, in chair) on the front veranda of the hotel. Daughter Hattie Crocker is to his immediate right; the other guests are friends of the family. (Courtesy of Pat Hathaway.)

Leland Stanford initially considered naming the hotel after himself, but Major R. P. Hammond, the Southern Pacific's chief civil engineer, persuaded him to name the hotel for the grove of magnificent trees that surrounded it. *Monte alto* is the Spanish phrase for woodland or forest, and the name Hotel del Monte was officially announced in the April 10, 1880, edition of the *Monterey Californian*. (Courtesy of author.)

David Jacks came to Monterey in 1850. A Scottish immigrant, he purchased, finagled, and foreclosed on thousands of acres in the county. The PIC bought 7,000 acres of land that made up the park reservation (today's Del Monte Forest) from him. The actual site of the hotel belonged to the Toomes family and was purchased in a referee's sale. (Photograph by I. W. Taber; courtesy of Pat Hathaway.)

Crocker hired Arthur Brown, chief civil engineer of the Central Pacific Railroad, to design the seaside resort hotel. Brown's architectural experience included the design and building of Crocker's Nob Hill mansion. Brown's son, Arthur Brown Jr., followed in his father's successful footsteps and is often erroneously credited with the design of the Hotel del Monte. He was only six years old when it was built in 1880. (Courtesy of author.)

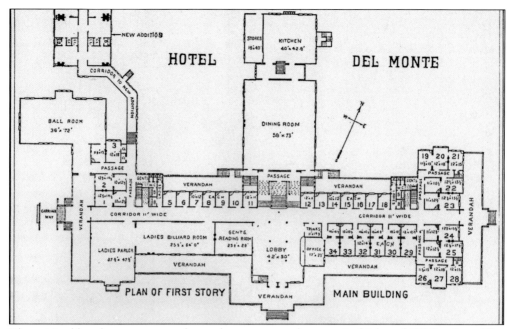

The original hotel was a mammoth wooden structure, three stories high and 385 feet long. The ballroom floor was made of inlaid wood, and a dozen chandeliers hung along the central corridor. Described architecturally as "modern Gothic" in style, the hotel was compared to the "famous Buckingham Palace." Approximately 400 guests could be accommodated if the single gentlemen didn't mind doubling up in the tower rooms. (Courtesy of author.)

Crocker intended the grounds of the hotel to be one of its main attractions. A rose garden flanked the southeastern front of the hotel, and a large sandbox for children to play in was placed close by. The tall Monterey pines to the left in this photograph were part of the original grove of trees standing on the property before the hotel was built. (Photograph by I. W. Taber; courtesy of author.)

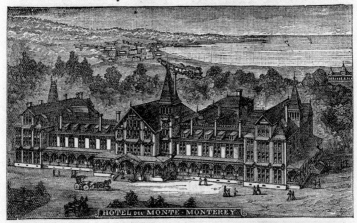
This 1883 advertisement placed in *Harper's Magazine Advertiser* comprehensively covered all of the hotel's attractions. First and foremost, Crocker decided that it should be open to tourists in the summer and "health-seekers" in the winter. This was proof indeed of California's superior climate, an important point to the owners, who were inveterate boosters of the state. Around 25 miles of macadamized road were developed for driving, encompassing beautiful scenery and historical sights. Both ocean bathing and swimming tanks at the bathhouse were available to guests, as was the 126-acre park that surrounded the hotel. All could be had for $3 a day, with special accommodations for bridal parties. (Courtesy of author.)

13

Monterey is 125 miles south of San Francisco. Crocker ordered powerful locomotives that could make the trip in just three and a half hours. The Monterey Express, called the Daisy Train by local residents, was scheduled to leave Monterey at 6:22 a.m. and return from San Francisco at 7:35 p.m. (Photograph by C. K. Tuttle; courtesy of Pat Hathaway.)

A small, gingerbread-trimmed train depot was built along the county road bordering Monterey Bay, a quarter mile from the hotel. Guests descending from the train boarded an elegant horse-drawn wagon, while their luggage rode in a separate conveyance. Up to 500 pieces of luggage per day were handled when the hotel was full. (Courtesy of author.)

George Schonewald managed Lick House in San Francisco before he was hired in January 1880 to run the as yet unbuilt Hotel del Monte. His wife, Katharine, assumed the position of housekeeper. Schonewald worked as a confectioner and a cook when he first came to California, and guests considered it a special privilege to be invited to the Schonewalds' private dining room. (Courtesy of author.)

Rudolph Ulrich (center) was hired to superintend the grounds shortly after the hotel opened. A highly skilled landscape gardener, he trained in Europe before coming to America in 1868. Ulrich lived with his wife and four children in a cottage above the cutting gardens. He remained with the hotel until 1890. (Courtesy of author.)

Many guests spent a great deal of time on the veranda, chatting or simply gazing out into the park. This fellow must have gotten up mighty early to read in peace and quiet, with only the birds in the trees and the muted roar of the surf for company. (Photograph by O. V. Lange; courtesy of Special Collections, Stanford University.)

Ulrich created two enormous, rectangular flower beds on each side of the front steps. Foundation plants were massed naturally below the railing, in contrast to the highly stylized carpet beds that filled the center of each plat. Ulrich alternated between planting elaborate abstract designs and spelling out homilies within the center beds. (Photograph by O. V. Lange; courtesy of Special Collections, Stanford University.)

The eastern wing of the building held 20 guest rooms. Among them was Charles Crocker's preferred room, No. 27. The windows on the upper floors overlooked the East Gardens and Laguna del Rey. (Photograph by O. V. Lange; courtesy of Special Collections, Stanford University.)

Ulrich laid out the East Gardens in 1884. They consisted of a series of three terraced areas that led down to the small lake where boats were kept for the use of guests. From the eastern veranda, one could see out over a broad roadway to the first terrace. A glimpse of Laguna del Rey is visible in the background. (Photograph by O. V. Lange; courtesy of Special Collections, Stanford University.)

The hotel proved so popular that thousands of guests were turned away due to insufficient space. An addition, seen here, was constructed in 1883 and provided 64 more rooms. Even so, lack of accommodations continued to be a problem. The addition was connected to the western end of the hotel by a long, curving corridor. (Photograph by I. W. Taber; courtesy of Pat Hathaway.)

One of the most popular "floral devices" created by Ulrich was the 1886 Grand Army Badge, intended to commemorate the 40th anniversary of the United States' victory over Mexico. The central emblem measured 33 feet by 24 feet. Ulrich planted this patriotic design in a plat of grass across from the clubhouse. (Photograph by C. W. J. Johnson; courtesy of author.)

The clubhouse contained a bar, a bowling alley, and a smoking room. It faced the road that ran between the hotel and stable, and was very much the private men's retreat. (Photograph by I. W. Taber; courtesy of Pat Hathaway.)

The bathing pavilion, or bathhouse, was a cavernous building sited on the beach about a half mile from the hotel. Four steam-heated tanks held a total of 450,000 gallons of sea water that was changed daily. The ridgeline of the roof was paned with glass, and there were approximately 200 dressing rooms. The construction cost was $75,000. (Courtesy of author.)

Crocker and Stanford both loved racing trotting horses, and Stanford had an extremely successful training facility set up at his Palo Alto estate. Crocker was seriously injured as a result of an accident while racing bank president D. O. Mills in New York. The inclusion of a racetrack for the guest's entertainment was inevitable, given these two gentlemen's interest in prime horseflesh. (Courtesy of author.)

These two engravings were included in one of the very first souvenir pamphlets available to guests. Hallmarks of Ulrich's landscaping—the use of climbing roses on trees and placing exotic plants as focal points within the grounds—can be seen in these two views. (Courtesy of author.)

Monterey's mild climate and Ulrich's lush landscaping combined to provide "midwinter" views that were used to promote California's superior natural resources. While crossing the country by rail, Eastern tourists were amazed to leave the snow behind from one day to the next. This engraving is based on a photograph by C. T. Watkins. (Courtesy of author.)

ARIZONA GARDEN — CACTI 13 FT HIGH.

The crown jewel of the many different gardens found on the hotel grounds was the Arizona Garden. Because 19th-century tourists had little opportunity to view such exotic plants, they were awed by the imposing saguaros. Ulrich's use of desert plants in a formal design was unique. This engraving appeared in an 1887 edition of *Harper's Weekly*. (Courtesy of author.)

The formal aspect of Ulrich's design can be seen in this view of the Arizona Garden, taken from the rooftop of the nearby aviary. A total of 17 people are posing among the 58 beds. Ulrich collected and brought plants from the Sonoran Desert, between the Arizona Territory and Mexico, using a locomotive, boxcars, a crew of men, and wagons with several teams of horses. The rail connection provided by the owners was crucial to the creation of this unique garden. The November 3, 1881,

Salinas Weekly Index reported, "Mr. Ulrich, the head gardener of the Del Monte Hotel, returned on Wednesday last from a trip to Mexico, where he has been to purchase plants indigenous to that country. One carload of cactus and other tropical plants has already arrived and three more are expected next week." (Photograph by I. W. Taber; courtesy of author.)

Ulrich used a German style of carpet bedding known as *teppichgartnerei* to decorate many of the plats within the Arizona Garden. These elaborate designs utilized many different sorts of plants. Flowing lines of rocks and shells were used to accentuate the patterns. (Courtesy of author.)

One of the most popular plants of the Victorian era was pampas grass. Here two guests seated in a wheelbarrow pose in front of an impressive specimen. Part of the aviary, which housed golden pheasants and other game birds, can be seen in the background. (Courtesy of Pat Hathaway.)

Two of the Chinese gardeners can be seen standing near a guest. Schonewald outraged the editor of the *Monterey Californian* in August 1880, when he discharged all of the white gardeners and kept the Chinese. Schonewald believed that seven Chinese would do the work of 14 white men. Anti-Chinese sentiment was virulent in 19th-century California. (Photograph by I. W. Taber; courtesy of Pat Hathaway.)

The most intriguing plant found in the Arizona Garden was the saguaro. This 13-foot specimen was probably around 75 years old when Ulrich brought it back from the Sonoran Desert in 1881. (Courtesy of Pat Hathaway.)

The coast live oaks found in the original grove of trees surrounding the hotel were an important feature of the hotel's landscape. Their imposing presence gave the nascent gardens an immediate sense of age and timelessness. (Photograph by R. Arnold; courtesy of Pat Hathaway.)

Ulrich trained ivy to climb up the trunks of the oaks and pines that filled the park. Crocker wrote to Huntington that he thought the site "was the prettiest place for a hotel that I know of and the old forest trees around it look beautiful." (Photograph by C. T. Watkins; courtesy of author.)

Guests take an opportunity to lounge on the veranda rail while admiring the floral work below. Ulrich changed the patterns of these carpet beds seasonally. Maintenance of the carpet beds, which were planted throughout the grounds, was extremely labor intensive. (Photograph by C. W. J. Johnson; courtesy of Pat Hathaway.)

A governess and her young charge pose on a bench in the South Gardens, directly in front of the hotel. Flowers line the pathway, their fragrance filling the air. Ulrich used plants from around the world, many of which bloomed in California's wintertime. (Photograph by C. W. J. Johnson; courtesy of Pat Hathaway.)

Walks through the grounds were made more interesting by the many and varied types of plantings. Several curvilinear pathways ran through the South Gardens, flowing around the mature oaks and pines whenever necessary. (Photograph by C. T. Watkins; courtesy of Pat Hathaway.)

Three lawn tennis courts (later resurfaced with bitumen) were laid out within the South Gardens. The carpet beds seen above featured rare exotics as their centerpieces; these were known as "dot" plants due to their prominent position. (Photograph by C. W. J. Johnson; courtesy of author.)

Here is a classic example of Ulrich's use of *teppichgartnerei* within the grass plats. He typically used a blend of succulents and herbaceous plants for each design, with an emphasis on texture and color. Plants were hand trimmed with scissors to keep them uniform in appearance. (Photograph by C. W. J. Johnson; courtesy of Pat Hathaway.)

The owners intended the hotel for family use and included many amenities for small children. Wooden swings, such as the one pictured here, along with slides, sandboxes, and teeter-totters, were placed throughout the grounds. (Photograph by C. W. J. Johnson; courtesy of Pat Hathaway.)

Three children stand on a pathway in the South Gardens. A rope swing hangs from a tree bough to the left, and one of the two croquet grounds can be seen at the far left. (Photograph by C. W. J. Johnson; courtesy of Pat Hathaway.)

The use of lawn in 1880s California was restricted to large private estates and parks such as the one found at the Hotel del Monte. Water for irrigation was scarce and the Mediterranean climate provided no rainfall for months at a time. Ulrich maintained 75 acres of velvety lawn within the 126-acre park. (Photograph by C. T. Watkins; courtesy of author.)

Driving was one of the chief entertainments available to guests. Wealthy visitors who stayed for a season often brought their own carriages and horses with them. These were housed in a large stable built on the western edge of the property. (Photograph by C. W. J. Johnson; courtesy of Pat Hathaway.)

Roads intended for driving were laid out within the park. One favored drive was the road that completely encircled Laguna del Rey, which lay along the county road. The lake's fountain can be seen in the background. (Photograph by C. W. J. Johnson; courtesy of Pat Hathaway.)

Laguna del Rey was a natural marsh dredged to create an 11-acre lake. When the hotel opened in June 1880, it was christened Lake Como, and rowboats supplied to guests were called gondolas in an attempt to evoke the Italian Riviera. The name was used for only a few months before the lake was dubbed Laguna del Rey. (Photograph by R. Arnold; courtesy of Pat Hathaway.)

Three stylish ladies pose behind two toddlers in a wicker perambulator along the edge of the lake. This area was barren before Ulrich planted the trees and flowering shrubbery along the shoreline. (Courtesy of Pat Hathaway.)

A small boat landing was built directly in line with the East Gardens, connecting the hotel with Laguna del Rey. The railing of the landing matched that of the hotel verandas. Two boats float placidly on the quiet water. (Photograph by R. Arnold; courtesy of Pat Hathaway.)

Ulrich planted willows, palm trees, and this short allée of dracaenas along the curving pathway of the lake. The *Dracaena draco*, or dragon tree, was an another extremely popular plant of the Victorian era. Rocks line the walkway. (Photograph by R. Arnold; courtesy of Pat Hathaway.)

Feeding the black and white swans was a favorite pastime. A flock of turkeys also roamed the grounds. Guests can be seen rowing in the background. The hotel orchestra would play for boaters from the landing on moonlit evenings. (Courtesy of author.)

Several small islands were built up for use as avian nesting grounds. One tiny mound, on the far side of the lake, was called a "fairy island." One very large tree and a small rock grotto left very little room for guests to walk around. The island was reached by a long wooden pier. (Courtesy of author.)

One of the recreations provided for the guests was a croquet plat, laid out within the South Gardens. Candles could be placed on top of the goal posts to allow play at night. One of the lawn tennis courts is visible in the background. (Photograph by C. W. J. Johnson; courtesy of Pat Hathaway.)

Lawn tennis was an extremely popular sport, introduced to North America in 1874. Three lawn courts were set up between the Arizona Garden and the maze. The lowest terrace of the East Gardens was transformed from a children's playground into a proper tennis court for tournament play. (Photograph by C. W. J. Johnson; courtesy of Pat Hathaway.)

Ulrich designed and planted a maze in 1885. The main entrance was flanked with Italian cypress trees and dahlias. The night watchman kept a ladder nearby to assist hopelessly lost guests over the cypress walls. Local boys from town earned pocket money by offering to lead guests back to civilization; they were tipped for their welcomed assistance. (Courtesy of Pat Hathaway.)

The hedge maze was created with Monterey cypress, and topiary chess pieces adorned the tops of the walls. As the maze matured, the walls grew to a thickness of four feet; interior hedges reached seven feet high. The center of the maze can be seen at the far left of this photograph. It took two men a month to hand trim the entire structure. (Courtesy of author.)

Situated on the eastern edge of the South Gardens, the maze had four corner outlets in addition to the main entrance. It was a half-mile walk from the entrance to the center, not counting wrong turns. Hotel staff provided colored bits of paper for guests to strew in their wake but they still got lost. (Courtesy of Pat Hathaway.)

Here is a plan of the Hotel del Monte maze. It was very similar to the one at Hampton Court, though the English maze did not have any chess pieces on the walls. The white areas at the bottom are the large flower beds that flanked the main entrance. (Photograph by R. Arnold; courtesy of Pat Hathaway.)

This is an extremely rare photograph taken by a guest who actually reached the much-sought center of the maze. Supposedly, a wooden viewing platform was built here when the maze was first planted, allowing successful guests to watch and direct their friends to the goal. Only benches can be seen in this image. (Courtesy of author.)

Military groups from the nearby Presidio and from San Francisco often camped in the grove on the hotel grounds. In 1880, Crocker organized a Fourth of July parade made up of militia members and hotel guests. The event was depicted in this painting entitled "Camp Crocker." (Photograph by J. P. Graham; courtesy of Monterey Public Library.)

Live music was integral to 19th century culture. The Monterey City Band was closely involved with many of the holiday celebrations held at the Hotel del Monte and was part of the lively exchange of social activities between the hotel and the town. The hotel was open 365 days a year, and every holiday was observed with fancy dinners, grand balls, fireworks, and impromptu parades. (Photograph by C. W. J. Johnson; courtesy of Pat Hathaway.)

Wealthier guests arrived in stylish private passenger cars that sat on sidings at the depot until the return trip home. Many times passengers slept in their own cars if rooms were unavailable. When millionaire William K. Vanderbilt arrived in his fancy Pullman, guests flocked to admire his elaborately appointed transportation. (Photograph by C. W. J. Johnson; courtesy of Pat Hathaway.)

The bustle found at the Del Monte train depot is apparent in this photograph taken during the 1890s. The Southern Pacific would run special additional trains when the hotel was particularly crowded due to a grand ball or holiday celebration. (Photograph by C. W. J. Johnson; courtesy of Pat Hathaway.)

This beautiful pair of matched horses may have belonged to the guests or to the hotel stable. The stable could accommodate 60 horses and as many carriages. (Photograph by C. W. J. Johnson; courtesy of Pat Hathaway.)

The hotel stable maintained a string of ponies and burros for children to ride and drive about the grounds. Here a group poses in front of the barn, which was close to the carriage house and Ulrich's nursery. Rental facilities in Monterey and Pacific Grove also provided horses and rigs for guests and tourists. (Photograph by C. W. J. Johnson; courtesy of Pat Hathaway.)

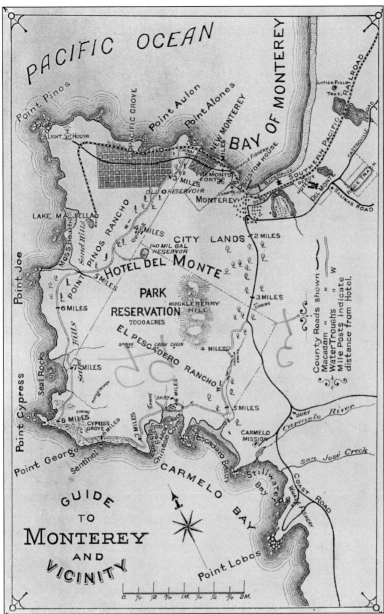

The owners of the hotel began constructing a scenic roadway for the guests' entertainment in late June 1880, using Chinese labor. By July 24, 1880, the *Monterey Californian* reported, "The wagon road around the beach to Point Cypress is now in splendid condition. It is a delightful drive out there." The road, initially referred to as Cypress Drive, was later called both 18-Mile Drive and 19-Mile Drive in early hotel pamphlets. The name 17-Mile Drive was finally settled on at some point in the 1890s. The road started at the front of the hotel, went through Monterey and Pacific Grove, then along spectacular coastline and through the Del Monte Forest. Various picnic spots and water troughs were set out along the winding roadway. The final destination was the Carmel Mission before the route swung back toward the hotel grounds, ending where it started at the resort's main entry. The trip was intended to last several hours and was considered the highlight of a stay at the Hotel del Monte. Hotel staff provided tourists with this map. (Courtesy of author.)

Guests could travel 17-Mile Drive on their own or in large, guided groups. Many people who were not registered guests at the hotel would show up on Sunday afternoons just to participate in the scenic tour. (Photograph by R. Arnold; courtesy of Pat Hathaway.)

One of the historic sights along the way was the Old Custom House. First built c. 1814, under Spanish rule, it was enlarged in 1822–1823 after the Mexican Empire was established. During this period, the arrival of foreign ships in the port was celebrated here with fancy balls. It is believed to be the oldest public building along the Pacific Coast. (Photograph by O. V. Lange; courtesy of Special Collections, Stanford University.)

These three carriages are on the portion of 17-Mile Drive running through Monterey and heading for Pacific Grove. The unpaved streets, wooden buildings, and old adobes seen here were typical of Monterey during the 1880s. (Photograph by C. W. J. Johnson; courtesy of Pat Hathaway.)

A few Chinese families lived on the hotel grounds near Laguna del Rey, but the majority of the Chinese population in the Monterey area resided in small villages along the coastline. Fishing was their main sustenance. The largest village, pictured here, was built on Point Alones (sometimes spelled Aulones), probably in the 1850s. The Hopkins Marine Station, part of Stanford University, now sits on this site. (Photograph by C. K. Tuttle; courtesy of Pat Hathaway.)

Pacific Grove Retreat was founded in 1875 by Methodist Episcopal clergymen intent on creating a campground where conditions were favorable to the health of body and soul. An association was formed and lots were sold, with half of the proceeds going to David Jacks to repay a $30,000 loan for improvements. After the association defaulted, Jacks sold the remaining land to the PIC. (Photograph by C. W. J. Johnson; courtesy of Pat Hathaway.)

Next stop along the tour was Point Pinos Lighthouse. Built in 1853–1854, it is the oldest continuously operating lighthouse on the Pacific coast. A third-order Fresnel light, with lenses, prisms, and mechanism manufactured in France, provided the necessary warning to ships entering Monterey Bay. (Photograph by C. W. J. Johnson; courtesy of Pat Hathaway.)

Moss Beach stretched out about a mile away from Pacific Grove. At low tide tourists could walk out nearly a half mile on hard packed sand. The beach was named for the forms of delicate sea mosses that washed up on shore during high tide. (Photograph by C. W. J. Johnson; courtesy of author.)

Point Joe was so named because local residents knew the man who lived there as "Chinaman Joe." He occupied a lean-to made of driftwood and recycled lumber and earned his living by raising goats and selling trinkets to the tourists. Singing softly to himself, Joe often walked between his home and Monterey with a cat riding on his shoulder. (Courtesy of Pat Hathaway.)

Seal Rock, near Fan Shell Beach, was home to hundreds of seals, as well as sea gulls, pelicans, and cormorants. (Photograph by C. W. J. Johnson; courtesy of Pat Hathaway.)

Fan Shell Beach boasted pure white sand and was a favored spot for seals bearing their young. The underwater reef there may have contributed to some of the shipwrecks that occurred in the area. (Photograph by L. Josselyn; courtesy of Pat Hathaway.)

Entering a grove of Monterey cypress, tourists were awed by these mysterious trees. How did they survive such harsh conditions? Why did they only grow naturally on the Monterey Peninsula? (Courtesy of Pat Hathaway.)

Beaten into fantastical shapes by the relentless wind, the trees were given whimsical names. Here is a group known as the Wizard Trees. (Courtesy of Pat Hathaway.)

Tourists pose beneath a noteworthy specimen. Native American Constanoans used a decoction of Monterey cypress leaves to treat rheumatism. (Courtesy of Pat Hathaway.)

Cypress Point was considered one of the highlights of 17-Mile Drive. It was here and at Point Lobos that the Monterey cypress grew naturally, always within a half mile of the high tide mark (Photograph by L. Josselyn; courtesy of Pat Hathaway.)

The Ostrich Tree, comprised of two cypress trees that grew together to form the large bird, stood on Cypress Point until both trees blew down in a storm in 1916. (Courtesy of Pat Hathaway.)

Cattle were grazed throughout the Del Monte Forest and were a common sight along 17-Mile Drive. (Photograph by C. W. J. Johnson; courtesy of Pat Hathaway.)

The Loop was laid out on a headland that jutted out into the water at or near Cypress Point. In this photograph, a horse and buggy pause at or near Cypress Point along the main drive. (Photo by C. K. Tuttle; courtesy of Pat Hathaway.)

This view of 17-Mile Drive was taken from the Loop. (Photograph by R. Arnold; courtesy of Pat Hathaway.)

One of the most photographed trees in the world is the Lone Cypress at Midway Point. An image of this tree appeared in the earliest hotel souvenir albums and pamphlets. The outcrop was initially referred to as Signal Rock. (Photograph by C. W. J. Johnson; courtesy of Pat Hathaway.)

Farther along 17-Mile Drive stood the Ghost Tree. This ancient cypress, quite dead but still standing resolute, was completely devoid of foliage. A young Chinese child can be seen leaning against an abalone shell stand across the road. Selling shells as souvenirs was another source of income for the Chinese fishing community. (Photograph by R. Arnold; courtesy of Pat Hathaway.)

This view from one of the picnic stops along 17-Mile Drive shows Point Lobos along the horizon across Carmel Bay. (Photograph by C. W. J. Johnson; courtesy of Pat Hathaway.)

Pebble Beach was a popular stop for picnics along the drive. (Photograph by C. W. J. Johnson; courtesy of Pat Hathaway.)

This photograph of a Chinese village was labeled "Pescadero. Cypress Drive." Today the area is known as Stillwater Cove. *Pescadero* is the Spanish word for "fishing place." (Photograph by C. W. J. Johnson; courtesy of Pat Hathaway.)

A Chinese person, bundled up against the chilly air, sits patiently behind a rough-hewn table supporting his wares. A neighbor or relative stands nearby. (Courtesy of Pat Hathaway.)

This rest stop along 17-Mile Drive provided a watering trough for the horses. (Courtesy of Pat Hathaway.)

The Carmel Mission was founded by Fr. Junipero Serra in June 1770. In 1880, when tourists first started visiting the abandoned mission, it was in ruins. Father Casanova, a priest who lived in Monterey, began raising funds for its restoration early that year. (Courtesy of author.)

Two

SECOND HOTEL
1887–1924

We have decided to commence the reconstruction of the hotel immediately.

—Col. C. Frederick Crocker

The Hotel del Monte caught fire near midnight of April 1, 1887, and burned to the ground within a few hours. No lives were lost. The dismissed hotel manager, E. T. M. Simmons, who had taken over from Schonewald in 1886, was charged with arson. He was completely exonerated at the court trial. Whether the fire was deliberately set or an accident is still unknown. (Photograph by C. W. J. Johnson; courtesy of Pat Hathaway.)

The PIC vowed to rebuild a new Hotel del Monte, one even bigger and better than before. They again hired Arthur Brown as the architect. Brown enlarged the footprint of the original structure and designed two flanking annexes to hold the majority of the guest rooms. These annexes were connected to the main structure by curving glass and iron "fireproof" arcades similar to the corridor that had tied the 1883 addition to the first hotel. Brown intended the arcades to

be used as firebreaks between the annexes and the main building. If fire broke out, they would be dynamited in hopes of saving part of the hotel. Construction proceeded quickly, though not quite at the phenomenal rate of 1880. Once again, all of the furnishings and appointments were of top quality. (Photograph by C. W. J. Johnson; courtesy of Pat Hathaway.)

The PIC was already building the Hotel del Carmelo at Pacific Grove when the fire occurred. The "sister" hotel was consequently rushed to completion, and guests who did not want to cancel their Hotel del Monte reservations stayed at El Carmelo. The name was later changed to the Pacific Grove Hotel to avoid mail delivery problems with nearby Carmel. (Photograph by C. W. J. Johnson; courtesy of Pat Hathaway.)

New engravings were created to advertise the reopening of the Hotel del Monte. The fireproof arcades were prominently displayed, as were the new gardens designed by Ulrich. He had extended the landscaping around the hotel to include the service court area, thus giving each guestroom in the annexes a garden view. (Courtesy of author.)

A Thanksgiving luncheon was served in the new dining room of the Hotel del Monte on Thursday, November 24, 1887. This was followed by a program of music performed by the Del Monte Band and a ball. However the hotel was not yet ready for overnight guests. Rooms did not become available until December 8, 1887. (Photograph by R. Arnold; courtesy of Pat Hathaway.)

The front section of the South Gardens was completely ruined by the fire and subsequent construction. After months of being trampled on and used as storage space for building materials, the plats were quickly restored to their former splendor. These carpet beds were intended to be viewed from the upper stories of the hotel as well as at ground level. (Photograph by I. W. Taber; courtesy of author.)

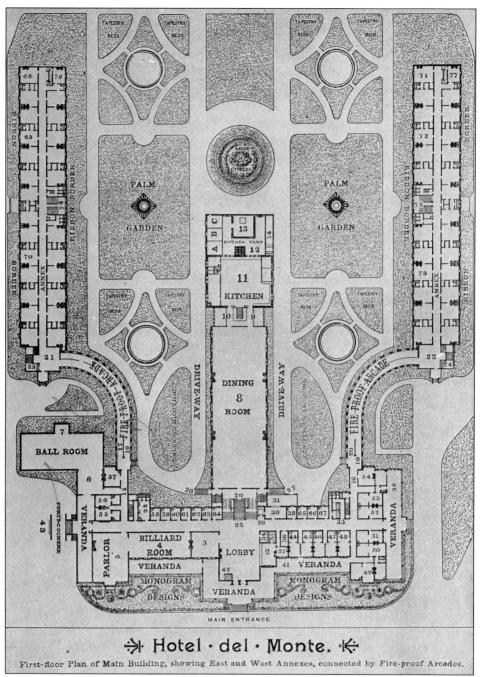

⇥ Hotel · del · Monte. ⇤

First-floor Plan of Main Building, showing East and West Annexes, connected by Fire-proof Arcades.

This floor plan of the second Hotel del Monte illustrated the new landscaping as well as the new buildings. Although a symmetrical garden is shown in the service court, photographs tell a different story. The two circular areas at the top of the page were intended to be fountains, but were instead planted as elaborate carpet beds. The lower circle on the right, as well as the adjacent area marked "Coniferous grouping," were eliminated completely to facilitate wagon deliveries. Though not strictly representative of the landscaping, the floor plan was accurate in its depiction of the buildings and their interiors. (Courtesy of author.)

60

Ghosts at the Hotel del Monte? Rumors have abounded for years; a man in an old-fashioned gray suit, a face peering in through a ballroom window, and other apparitions have reportedly haunted the hotel and grounds. Here several phantoms appear to have dropped into the lobby for a cozy chat amongst themselves before returning to their various self-appointed rounds. (Photograph by R. Arnold; courtesy of Pat Hathaway.)

In addition to the requisite tables, the ladies' billiard room held an open fireplace faced with English tiles depicting Shakespearean scenes. Large ornate mirrors hung on the walls. Apparently, men were allowed to play here as well as at the clubhouse, but the ladies did not intrude beyond the veranda of the men's sanctuary. (Photograph by C. W. J. Johnson; courtesy of Pat Hathaway.)

The pristine white dining room was lit by 164 gaslights and warmed by four large fireplaces, each faced with brightly colored English tiles showing floral motifs. Around 800 people could be seated at one time. White linen graced the tables, and the china was made to order in Limoges, France. The glassware consisted of 7,520 pieces, plus an additional 177,492 porcelain items. (Photograph by C. W. J. Johnson; courtesy of Pat Hathaway.)

The Hotel del Monte prided itself on its cuisine. The menu was extensive and varied, and the wait staff paid particular attention to the needs of the guests. Here the kitchen and dining room personnel pose in the service court, adjacent to their respective work areas. The kitchen boasted the latest appliances, including ranges shipped from New York City. (Photograph by C. W. J Johnson; courtesy of Pat Hathaway.)

The front steps of the main entrance were a popular place to relax and bask in the sunshine. The grove of trees surrounding the hotel cast a fair amount of shade over the grounds; the only truly open areas were those immediately around the hotel, the East Garden terraces, the Arizona Garden, and the maze. (Courtesy of Pat Hathaway.)

Roses were one of Ulrich's favorite flowers. He planted 90 varieties in two separate rose gardens on the grounds, one near the maze and the other laid out in front of the southeastern end of the hotel. He also trained climbing roses up the front of the veranda, pictured here. (Photograph by R. Arnold; courtesy of Pat Hathaway.)

The verandas of the second hotel were enclosed with glass, unlike the open air porches of th first building. Potted plants, comfortable rocking chairs, and a small upright piano were part c the furnishings. Live music was a staple of the hotel's entertainment and could be heard in th form of impromptu concerts held on the veranda or formal evening programs. (Photograph b R. Arnold; courtesy of Pat Hathaway.)

Conventions took place regularly at the Hotel del Monte, although they were never booke during the fashionable months of March, July, and August. In 1896, when a group of hotelier toured California, George Wharton James wrote of the event, "No place in California did th HMMBA expect more than at Del Monte, and at no place were they more pleased and bette satisfied." (Photograph by R. Arnold; courtesy of Pat Hathaway.)

Touring the pathways and roads of the 126-acre park was a favored pastime. Here a trio of adults plans a leisurely spin while a child and another adult look on. (Courtesy of Pat Hathaway.)

Plants imported from around the world thrived under Ulrich's supervision. A collection of trees from nearly every country adorned the grounds, along with numerous exotic flowers and shrubs. Interest in horticulture was strong during the late 19th century, and guests often chose to be photographed standing near botanical specimens like this enormous feather palm. (Courtesy of author.)

A reporter from the *Boston Home Journal* wrote, "The Hotel del Monte is the most beautiful hotel I ever saw. I can see one hundred acres of lawn and flowers from my window, while the air is fragrant with the perfume of roses, violets, heliotropes, and other flowers." (Photograph by R. Arnold; courtesy of Pat Hathaway.)

Three guests stroll along a main drive dappled by the umbrageous oaks and pines. A buggy is parked nearby in the shade, and other vehicles can be seen grouped about the main entrance. (Courtesy of Pat Hathaway.)

Nature meets technology in the form of a gas-lit lamppost entwined with roses. The grounds were also illuminated by thousands of Japanese paper lanterns strung up on tree limbs for special evening festivities. (Photograph by C. W. J. Johnson; courtesy of Pat Hathaway.)

Benches were placed throughout the grounds for the convenience of the guests. Here a nattily attired gentleman poses for a portrait, his shoes shined and his umbrella tightly furled. (Photograph by C. W. J. Johnson; courtesy of Pat Hathaway.)

Ulrich dug up ferns from the nearby Del Monte Forest and transplanted them to the hotel grounds. (Courtesy of Pat Hathaway.)

The porte-cochere attached to the western veranda of the hotel was a covered porch through which carriages could be driven. Staff delivered luggage to this point from the train depot, and guests wishing to avoid the rain could alight from their carriage beneath the sheltering roof. (Courtesy of author.)

The grass plats that flanked the pathway to the clubhouse were heavily planted with trees. (Photograph by R. Arnold; courtesy of Pat Hathaway.)

At the same time the second Hotel del Monte was being built, the clubhouse was expanded. A similar building housing a large billiard hall and several private lunchrooms was erected adjacent to the original structure. The bowling alley was also improved. (Photograph by C. W. J. Johnson; courtesy of Pat Hathaway.)

Ulrich landscaped the monogram bed beneath the clubhouse veranda in a style similar to those found in front of the hotel. In addition to the abstract designs, he would also spell out floral greetings such as "To All And Each A Fair Welcome" or "Entrez Messieurs." (Photograph by C. T. Watkins; courtesy of author.)

A family touring the grounds by burro pauses by the clubhouse. (Photograph by C. W. J. Johnson courtesy of Pat Hathaway.)

Guests posing for photographs on the grounds had their choice of beautiful sites. Many favored the exotic Arizona Garden or the maze as a backdrop, but others were content with the ubiquitous lawn and trees. (Photograph by C. W. J. Johnson; courtesy of Pat Hathaway.)

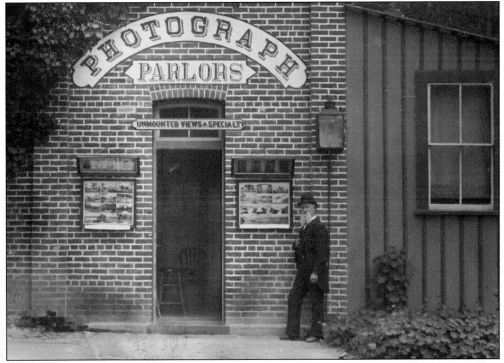

Charles Wallace Jacob Johnson was a man of many talents. In addition to being a gifted photographer, he was a musician and dance instructor. Here he stands in front of his photographic parlor, part of a brick-faced structure built close to the western end of the hotel in 1887. Examples of his views can be seen in frames on the wall. (Courtesy of Pat Hathaway.)

St. John's Chapel was built in 1891 by the English-trained architect Ernest Coxhead. Designed in the Shingle style, it evoked a sense of fantasy unusual in an ecclesiastical structure. The beautiful hotel grounds evoked a feeling of pastoral innocence that was particularly appropriate as a setting for this building. (Photograph by C. K. Tuttle; courtesy of Pat Hathaway.)

The interior of the chapel was a perfect complement to the fairytale exterior. The miniature scale of the space and its contents was beautifully realized. (Photograph by C. W. J. Johnson; courtesy of Pat Hathaway.)

The hotel had been a favorite of honeymooners since it first opened in 1880. Once the chapel was built, it became a preferred site for weddings as well. (Photograph by R. Arnold; courtesy of Pat Hathaway.)

Pebble Beach was as popular throughout the 1890s as it had been in the preceding decade. Guests enjoyed picking up the agates and water drops worn smooth by the ocean's constant motion. When the water stirred the stones, a distinct shushing sound could be heard. (Photograph by C. K. Tuttle; courtesy of Pat Hathaway.)

President Benjamin Harrison and his retinue visited the Hotel del Monte in 1891. Touring 17-Mile Drive by coach, the party stopped close by the Loop. One of the passengers seated in the back can be seen turning to peer over his shoulder at the presidential photographer. (Courtesy of Special Collections, Stanford University.)

A member of Harrison's group stands in the Arizona Garden. The entire party spent the night and one full day at the hotel. On their second night, everyone slept in the presidential train at the depot to facilitate an early start back to San Francisco. (Courtesy of Special Collections, Stanford University.)

Ulrich treated the bathhouse as a conservatory, and tropical plants flourished in the steamy atmosphere. The containers of the large palms seen here had wheels and could be rolled out to sit on the walls that divided the tanks. (Photograph by C. K. Tuttle; courtesy of Pat Hathaway.)

Guests and hotel workers cavort in the empty swimming tanks. The man standing on the far right is wearing the required bathing costume of the day, a one-piece suit that covered his body from the neck to the knees. Women wore a similar getup, but with the addition of a skirt and long black stockings to cover bare legs. (Photograph by C. W. J. Johnson; courtesy of Pat Hathaway.)

Fashionable tennis clubs kept the courts at the Hotel del Monte occupied, and the horse racing and polo groups were similarly engaged out at the track. (Courtesy of author.)

An entirely new sport was introduced to the guests with the completion of the nine-hole Del Monte Golf Course in 1897. Equally popular with both men and women, the course was designed by English-born Charlie Maud. The beautiful oaks already growing on the site were left in place. These photographs, found in an 1899 hotel pamphlet, are some of the earliest images available of golfing at Hotel del Monte. (Courtesy of author.)

Richard Arnold became the hotel's second official photographer after Charles Johnson retired in the late 1890s. He was interested in early California photography and had amassed his own collection of images. His studio was in Monterey, at the corner of Alvarado and Pearl Streets, rather than on the hotel grounds. (Courtesy of Pat Hathaway.)

Schonewald and Arthur Brown were both present when the gas was lit up for the first time in the second hotel by foreman Mike Dorgan. A *Monterey Argus* reporter wrote, "The immense building, one blaze of light, was a grand spectacle, and to one standing in the grounds it was hard to realize that the disastrous scenes of the night of April 1st were really enacted." (Courtesy of Monterey Public Library.)

The 60-foot plume of water produced by the fountain in Laguna del Rey could be seen by passengers of the Del Monte Express as it passed along the edge of the grounds. Water was first made available for the fountain in the fall of 1883, after the PIC constructed a pipeline from the Carmel River to a 147-million-gallon reservoir in Monterey. Chinese labor was used for the arduous project, as it had been for the grading of 17-Mile Drive. A plentiful supply of pure water

had been a problem since the hotel first opened in 1880, but it was deemed too expensive an improvement at an estimated cost of $30,000. The success of the hotel forced the issue as the amount of water supplied by an artesian well on the grounds was wholly inadequate. (Courtesy of Monterey Public Library.)

Another presidential visit was made to the hotel in 1903. Theodore Roosevelt, whose party had the entire East Annex to themselves for security reasons, thoroughly enjoyed the scenic 17-Mile Drive. Astride a powerful black mare, Roosevelt galloped much of the distance in 90 minutes flat, leaving his Secret Service men in the dust. Upon his return, he asked, "Any chance for a hunting trip this afternoon?" (Courtesy of Pat Hathaway.)

By 1904, the emphasis on outdoor activities for guests was clearly stated in the hotel's letterhead. "Polo, Automobiling and Golf the year round" was printed underneath a photographic banner of guests at play. (Courtesy of author.)

Hotel Del Monte

By the Sea—Near Old Monterey

All out-door sports—golf, tennis, surf and pool bathing; glass bottom boats. Full eighteen hole golf course—the best in the world. Oiled roads for auto rides. Old Monterey with its historic adobes; The Presidio with its attractive military features; Pacific Grove with its shells and its cypresses, and Carmel bay with its Mission and its sandy beach are all close by. Special terms for families. Delightful out of doors every day in the year.

Address   **GEO. P. SNELL**
Manager Hotel Del Monte
DEL MONTE, CALIFORNIA

ON THE GOLF LINKS AT DEL MONTE

An advertisement for the Hotel del Monte lists all outdoor sports as the primary reason for coming to visit. The Del Monte Golf Course, to which another nine holes had been added in 1903, is clearly ascendant in the range of attractions offered to guests. Horsepower of the old-fashioned kind is still the mode of travel used for 17-Mile Drive. (Courtesy of author.)

At Del Monte

California's beautiful *Winter and Summer Hotel.* *Weather is ideal the year round for surf-bathing, hunting, automobiling, polo and pony racing.* The United States report of minimum temperatures shows what a *delightful spot Del Monte is at all seasons of the year: January, 44.4 degrees; February, 46.1; March, 51.8; April, 52.2.*

The Golf Links—A full eighteen-hole course, with greens and tees always green,—are considered the finest in the States.

In touring California, visit and prolong your stay at this delightful resort

GEORGE P. SNELL
Manager

The mild weather found in both winter and summer is the focus of this Maxfield Parrish–style advertisement. For the first time, an automobile is seen traversing 17-Mile Drive, and two young caddies are illustrated toting enormous golf bags. Local boys earned pocket money by caddying and retrieving golf balls gone astray. (Courtesy of author.)

82

Now golf has moved up to the top of the page, quite literally. A horse-drawn carriage is shown in front of the hotel, but the automobile featured below the golfers is more prominently displayed. (Courtesy of author.)

Horse-drawn lawn mowers were still being used on the hotel grounds as late as 1916, but the newfangled steam-powered lawn mowers were cutting grass on the Del Monte Golf Course as soon as they hit the market. They spent more time in the repair shop than out on the turf. (Courtesy of Pat Hathaway.)

Golf and Hotel del Monte. Nothing more need be said in this 1906 ad. James Melville, one of the early golf pros hired by the hotel to teach the game, encouraged men, women, and children to play. His efforts established the Del Monte Golf Course as the center of golf in California. Melville was born in Scotland and learned the game at the Earl's Ferry Links. (Courtesy of author.)

Hotel Del Monte

DEL MONTE, CALIFORNIA.

OPEN ALL THE YEAR

THE FINEST GOLF LINKS IN THE WORLD.

Disaster struck Northern California on April 18, 1906, when the great earthquake began at 5:12 a.m. At the Hotel del Monte, one of the chimneys crashed through the roof, killing two people in room 97. They were Edward and Mary Rouzer of Arizona, and they had been married just 10 days earlier. Offered a choice of rooms, Mrs. Rouzer had picked the bridal suite that overlooked the South Gardens. (Courtesy of Pat Hathaway.)

In all, 25 of the hotel's chimneys collapsed or were damaged as a result of the earthquake. The PIC chose to remove them entirely rather than repair them. Here, two workers risk life and limb as they begin the laborious task of dismantling the brickwork. (Photograph by G. A. Quintel; courtesy of Pat Hathaway.)

A. D. Shepard, general manager of the PIC, came up with the idea of an art gallery at the Hotel del Monte. Knowing that San Francisco was in ruins after the earthquake and fire and that many artists were temporarily relocating to the Monterey Peninsula, he had the ballroom set up in 1907 so that the work of California artists was featured exclusively for the first time. (Photograph by R. Arnold; courtesy of Pat Hathaway.)

California was still considered a remote cultural backwater in 1907, and the display of fine paintings at the Hotel del Monte helped established the fact that California artists had strong ties with the eastern United States and Europe. One of the most significant styles of painting at the time was plein air, and the artists who utilized it were called American Luminists. Here is a painting of Monterey Bay. (Courtesy of Pat Hathaway.)

By mid-1907, automobiles had completely replaced horse-drawn carriages for tours of 17-Mile Drive. Guests now signed up and paid for chauffer-driven expeditions at a window on the hotel's front veranda. H. R. Warner, manager of the hotel, hired a local man to oversee the operation. This little boy seems somewhat apprehensive about the new mode of travel. (Courtesy of Pat Hathaway.)

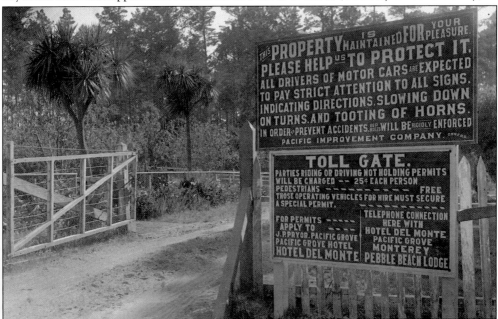

Signs warning of the dangers of driving were posted along 17-Mile Drive. Tolls were collected at the Forest Lodge Gate in Pacific Grove and later at the Pebble Beach Gate, which was hung with a board denoting the Del Monte Forest. A hexagonal toll house stood at the Carmel Hill Gate. (Photograph by R. Arnold; courtesy of Pat Hathaway.)

In addition to golf, tennis, polo, and horse racing, the Del Monte Dog Show became one of the highlights of the social season. Here exhibitors such as Miss Jennie Crocker of San Francisco (terriers) and Mrs. W. C. Ralston of Belmont (cocker spaniels) vied for silver cups and ribbons. (Courtesy of Pat Hathaway.)

In 1909, A. D. Shepard put plans into motion to sell "villa" lots in the Del Monte Forest, starting with the Pebble Beach area. To this end, he arranged for several new roads, including the Scenic Boulevard, to be graded. He ordered Warner to have an enormous sign erected at Pebble Beach advertising "information and literature on request of the Pacific Improvement Company." (Courtesy of Pat Hathaway.)

As part of the real estate endeavor, A. D. Shepard hired Lewis Hobart to design a rustic lodge made of pine logs at Pebble Beach. Warner personally oversaw the skinning and oiling of the logs and experimented with laying the logs to make the strongest building possible. (Photograph by Slevin; courtesy of Monterey Public Library.)

The interior of the lodge consisted of an assembly room, reception and dressing rooms, a kitchen, and a dining room. The chief features of the assembly room, or great hall, were the two stone fireplaces that flanked each end of the room and the abalone chandeliers. Warner arranged for a local blacksmith to fashion these custom-made hanging light fixtures. (Photograph by D. Freeman; courtesy of Pat Hathaway.)

Barbeques and seafood were the fare offered to guests, in addition to afternoon tea. Shepard had signs posted along 17-Mile Drive forbidding the "indiscriminate gathering of mussels, abalone and other sea foods [as] we shall need all of these substances, for proper entertainment of the public at Pebble Beach Tavern." Bay Lodge, Pine Lodge, and Ye Tavern–Pebble Beach were initial considerations for naming the lodge. (Photograph by D. Freeman; courtesy of Pat Hathaway.)

Warner persuaded Shepard to settle on Pebble Beach Lodge. Shepard finally agreed to the name reasoning that "each time we mention it, we advertise Pebble Beach, and people who may purchase land in the interim will speak of going to Pebble Beach Lodge more definitely than by saying Bay Lodge." Dan Freeman, a local photographer, stands beneath the pergola with two women. (Photograph by R. Arnold; courtesy of Pat Hathaway.)

Advertising for "Del Monte's Sporting Feast" highlighted the Pacific Coast Tennis Championship, a golf tournament, and the annual dog show. Auto rallies and races were also part of the package. A "scene of weekend parties" was promised in conjunction with the dog show. (Courtesy of Pat Hathaway.)

Auto racing had eclipsed horse racing for the time being. The roar of the engines replaced the thudding of hooves at the racetrack. Here the Stutz racing team watches from the sidelines. (Photograph by R. Arnold; courtesy of Pat Hathaway.)

NO VISIT TO CALIFORNIA IS COMPLETE UNLESS IT INCLUDES

HOTEL DEL MONTE

DEL MONTE, CALIFORNIA
Near Old Monterey, 125 miles south of San Francisco
ON MONTEREY BAY

THE RIVIERA *of* AMERICA
A Place Where It Is Summer All the Year
SOMETHING NEW EACH DAY FOR YOUR PLEASURE *and* COMFORT

GOLF ON THE FINEST EIGHTEEN-HOLE COURSE IN AMERICA, within three minutes' walk of the hotel — ALL GRASS GREENS. Forty miles of magnificent scenic boulevards for motoring over mountains, through forests, beside the sea, all within our own estate. Hot and cold ocean water baths, surf bathing, sailing and deep-sea fishing, marine gardens, tennis, archery, hunting in 10,000-acre mountain preserve; finest polo field in California; upland-forest horseback riding over fascinating trails; *Sleeping Porches;* perfect service; unequaled table; *American Plan Only;* $4.00, $5.00, $6.00 and $7.00 per day, according to room and number occupying same

UNDER SAME MANAGEMENT
PACIFIC GROVE HOTEL

Pacific Grove, Cal., two miles beyond Del Monte, also on Monterey Bay; good street car connections; clean, wholesome, efficient. Guests are entitled to enjoy Del Monte grounds and all Del Monte privileges and attractions. Rates $2.50, $3.00, $3.50 and $4.00 per day, according to room and number occupying same. American Plan. *Address H. R. WARNER, Manager, DEL MONTE, CAL.*

DEL MONTE

CALIFORNIA

Comparisons between the scenic beauty of Monterey and the Italian Riviera had been made deliberately by the PIC in 1880, when the Hotel del Monte first opened. This practice was continued in a 1911 advertisement for the hotel. (Courtesy of author.)

Repeated references were made to fountains and pools on the grounds of the Hotel del Monte, but the only visual evidence remaining today is this 1912 photograph taken by Floyd Tuttle. Glimpses of the east veranda and east annex are just visible through the trees. (Courtesy of Pat Hathaway.)

A hotel gardener puts both body and soul into his work, trimming the immense hedge that lined Cypress Row. The pathway paralleled the East Gardens, and this shrub was probably considered a piece of cake to maintain when compared to the chessmen of the maze. (Courtesy of Pat Hathaway.)

Samuel F. B. Morse was hired in 1915 to liquidate the PIC. Many of the assets, including the hotel, had been losing money for several years. Morse was an Easterner who attended Yale and captained its undefeated football team in 1906. Two years later, he made his first visit to the Hotel del Monte. His ebullient personality is captured in this photograph by Julian Graham. (Courtesy of Pat Hathaway.)

One of the first things Morse did with regard to the Hotel del Monte was to fire Warner and replace him with Carl Stanley, who ran the hotel until 1942. Stanley has been credited with turning the faltering hotel around within a year. Here he is with his family at Christmas, in the living room of the cottage now known as the Stanley House. (Courtesy of the Naval Postgraduate School.)

Morse hired Lewis Hobart, the same architect who had designed the first Pebble Beach Lodge, to plan the "Roman Plunge." The upper two terraces of the East Garden were replaced by the large pool with its columned solarium and a children's wading pool below it. The pools were extremely popular, and Hobart's work was featured in the distinguished journal *Architect and Engineer*. (Photograph by D. Freeman; courtesy of author.)

The rustic Pebble Beach Lodge burned down on December 26, 1917, following a holiday party held the night before. Because it had proven to be especially popular with the hotel's guests, Morse persuaded the PIC to let him rebuild, using salvaged lumber from the demolished Pacific Grove Hotel. The new lodge, opened in 1919, was the result of the combined efforts of Lewis Hobart and Clarence Tantau. (Courtesy of Pat Hathaway.)

The ocean side of the lodge shows a colonnade reminiscent of the Roman Plunge at the far left side of the building. Rooms for people to stay overnight were now available in addition to the cottages that had survived the blaze. The landscaping of the old lodge had included three acres of lawn that stretched down toward the water's edge. (Photograph by J. P. Graham; courtesy of Pat Hathaway.)

The living room, or terrace lounge, of the lodge provided guests with a place to relax and enjoy the view out over Carmel Bay toward Point Lobos. They also had something new to gaze upon: the Pebble Beach Golf Links. (Courtesy of author.)

Morse had envisioned Pebble Beach as a resort community identified with an incomparable golf course. He knew that improvements would accelerate real estate sales and thus convinced the PIC that the investment would pay for itself. He intended to preserve as much coastline as possible and so had the golf links laid out alongside it. (Photograph by C. Jones; courtesy of Pat Hathaway.)

One of Morse's economies was to employ sheep as greens keepers on the new course. This proved to be a short-lived experiment, however, as their sharp hooves indented the greens and fairways. Morse, anxious for Pebble Beach to earn the same respect as the Del Monte course, put Stanley in charge of bringing the new links up to a higher standard. (Photograph by L. Hugo; courtesy of Pat Hathaway.)

In 1918, an investor who showed interest in purchasing the PIC's Monterey assets spurred Morse to consider buying the property himself. He formed the Del Monte Properties Company in 1919, adopting the image of the Lone Cypress as his company trademark. He now owed the Hotel del Monte, the Del Monte Lodge (formerly Pebble Beach Lodge), two golf courses, property in Carmel Valley, and a water company. (Courtesy of author.)

Morse did not reinvent the wheel when it came to advertising his new holdings. The prose covered all of the usual highlights, from the mild climate to the luxurious lifestyle dominated by outdoor sports. (Courtesy of author.)

Three

THIRD HOTEL
1924–1942

As soon as the embers are cool, work will begin on our new building.

—S. F. B. Morse

Fire again broke out at the Hotel del Monte on September 27, 1924, and again no lives were lost. Firefighters, using TNT from the Presidio, dynamited the arcades, just as Arthur Brown had planned. This action spared the two annexes, although the central hotel building couldn't be saved. The *Peninsula Daily Herald* reported that a chimney spark near the main tower probably started the blaze. (Photograph by L. Josselyn; courtesy of Pat Hathaway.)

Two workers survey the smoldering wreckage the morning after the fire. Losses totaled nearly $3 million, but paintings valued at $75,000 were rescued from the art gallery. An estimated 2,500 people were on the grounds by dawn, many of them local residents who assisted with fighting the

"We kept the wings open and served meals in the quiet fall season over in the little golf grill This was only for a few weeks. The kitchen was intact, and we quickly built a building between the kitchen and the west wing, and connected the kitchen and the two wings. The new building was a canvas-covered runway. We moved the executive offices into the west wing and set up the

fire. Carl Stanley and his family lost all of their personal possessions, as did Mrs. Mary Quinby, a resident of the hotel since 1901. She was rescued by a hotel employee who found the doorway to her room engulfed in flames. (Photograph by A. C. Heidrick; courtesy of Pat Hathaway.)

hotel desk in the lobby of the west wing." Morse wrote this account of the period immediately following the fire in his unpublished memoir. (Photograph by A. C. Heidrick; courtesy of Pat Hathaway.)

The third Hotel del Monte is shown here under construction. Plans to build the new hotel in a "Spanish" style were reported in the newspaper the day of the fire. Morse again hired Lewis Hobart and Clarence Tantau as the architects. The wooden annexes were covered with stucco and re-roofed with red tiles to match the new hotel. (Courtesy of Pat Hathaway.)

The hotel cost $2 million to build and reopened on May 8, 1926. A lavish party, well-publicized in the usual Del Monte style, was attended by 3,500 "persons of note." The banquet began with fruit cup California and ended 16 courses later with patisserie, cafe noir, and mints. (Photograph by L. Josselyn; courtesy of Pat Hathaway.)

While the first two hotels had entrances that opened directly onto the main axis of the East Gardens, the third hotel was designed differently. Now, a single plate window, seen in the center of the photograph, simply overlooked the terraced area from the lobby. This window had to be custom-made due to its large dimensions. (Photograph by J. P. Graham; courtesy of Monterey Public Library.)

The sun terrace, placed on the west side of the main entrance, proved very popular with guests, who could seek shade under the umbrellas or covered gliders placed about the large porch, or toast themselves in the lounges set out in the full sun. It was a quiet area in comparison to the busy patio of the Roman Plunge. (Photograph by J. P. Graham; courtesy of Monterey Public Library.)

Elaborate scrollwork surrounds the doorway leading out to the sun terrace. Two urns flank the entrance. (Courtesy of author.)

Hobart had to redesign the landscape around the new hotel. He placed sunken gardens on each side of the central structure. The east side featured flower beds and the west side, pictured here, was planted out in lawn and shrubs. A small circular pool was placed in the middle of the courtyard. (Courtesy of author.)

An unbroken stretch of lawn that started below the enormous lobby window and merged with Ulrich's plat was another of Hobart's innovations. The monkey puzzle tree on the left and an edge of the bunya bunya tree seen at the far right were part of the original East Gardens. (Courtesy of author.)

The view from the lobby window took in the Roman Plunge and swept downward all the way to Laguna del Rey. (Courtesy of author.)

The lounge, equal in size to the lobby, had a large mural painted at each end of the room. Rendered by self-taught artist Daniel Groesbeck, the murals reflected California's Spanish heritage. This mural was entitled "Landing of the Cross" and shows Father Serra coming ashore in 1770, searching for Monterey Bay as described by Vizcaino after his 1602 discovery. (Courtesy of Monterey Public Library.)

Groesbeck's other mural was called "Building of the Missions" and depicted Native Americans working under the direction of Father Serra. A grand piano sits beneath the mural. Ornate rugs covered parts of the red-tiled floor and the ceiling was beautifully detailed. (Photograph by J. P. Graham; courtesy of Monterey Public Library.)

If the Victorian original was said to resemble a rich private estate, the effect Morse was striving for with the new Hotel del Monte was that of a country club. The lounge was furnished with comfortable upholstered sofas and chairs, scattered in groups throughout the large room. (Photograph by J. P. Graham; courtesy of Monterey Public Library.)

The two murals seen in the lobby were painted by local artist Francis McComas. This one is of the famed Monterey cypress. McComas was nationally known for his exquisite watercolors. His subjects included California oaks and cypresses and the American Southwest. (Photograph by J. P. Graham; courtesy of author.)

McComas begins work on the second mural in the lobby. A rough sketch of a Spanish galleon can be seen pinned up on the wall next to him. McComas was also an avid golfer and redesigned some portions of the original Pebble Beach Golf Links at Morse's request. (Photograph by J. P. Graham; courtesy of author.)

The "El Monte" mural depicted the Monterey Peninsula. McComas left off nearby Pacific Grove, supposedly as revenge after being arrested there for drinking. The Christian resort town had a strict policy of no alcohol and firmly refused the PIC's request to serve liquor at El Carmelo. (Photograph by J. P. Graham; courtesy of Monterey Public Library.)

The Hotel del Monte's tradition of fine cuisine and excellent service continued on in the "palatial" new dining room. Elaborate candelabras hung from the coffered Spanish Colonial ceiling and provided an "iridescent" twilight glow to the room. The absence of "reassuring pillars" used to support the 27-foot ceiling in such a large space (210 feet by 49 feet) was a noted architectural feat. (Photograph by J. P. Graham; courtesy of Monterey Public Library.)

Tile work was employed throughout the building, but nowhere was it more elaborately or beautifully utilized than in the fountain of the dining room. (Photograph by J. P. Graham; courtesy of Monterey Public Library.)

This photograph of the Tap Room is dated c. 1925, but in light of Prohibition it was probably not furnished as such until 1933. Not that Morse wasn't serving alcohol to his guests during the temperance era. He was, of course, but in a subtle fashion. Franklin D. Roosevelt's reversal of Prohibition was the only thing about his presidency of which Morse approved. (Photograph by J. P. Graham; courtesy of Monterey Public Library.)

Jo Mora, another local artist, created "La Novia" for the hotel's Copper Cup Room in 1940. This room, used for private banquets, was named for a cup kept in a niche in the wall. Mora included many authentic details in his sculpture of a groom carrying his bride homeward escorted by two friends. He also designed the cover art of many of the hotel menus. (Courtesy of Monterey Public Library.)

110

Morse was able to form Del Monte Properties Company by securing financing from Herbert Fleishhacker, president of San Francisco's Anglo Bank. Morse became president of DMPC and Fleishhacker was his major stockholder. Seen here is Fleishhacker's private suite at the new hotel, a perquisite, as was David Jacks's private entrance to the enclosed grounds. (Photograph by J. P. Graham; courtesy of Monterey Public Library.)

The guest bedrooms were furnished in a spare, yet elegant style. (Photograph by J. P. Graham; courtesy of Monterey Public Library.)

Much of the grounds remained unchanged. A broad road bisected the bottom of the East Gardens and the boat landing. The stairs leading up to the hotel were flanked with lawn, shrubs, trees, and urns. Pathways led off into the thick grove of trees that grew along each side of the East Garden terraces. (Photograph by J. P. Graham; courtesy of Monterey Public Library.)

A rock garden bounded the upper area of the boat landing, encompassed on each side by stairs that led up to the East Gardens. The edge of the garden and one set of stairs are in the foreground, and the pathway that encircled the lake heads off to the left toward the dracaena allée. (Photograph by J. P. Graham; courtesy of Monterey Public Library.)

Here is the maze c. 1920s. The hedge has been freshly trimmed and chess pieces still punctuate the tops of the walls. There are no flowers planted in the front bed, only grass and palm trees. (Photograph by J. P. Graham; courtesy of Monterey Public Library.)

Julian "Spike" Graham began working for Morse in 1924, shortly before the fire. While he photographed the guests as Johnson and Arnold had done in their day, he was particularly known for capturing "the thrill of the moment" in his action shots. Here he poses at the most notable landmark on the Monterey Peninsula, the Lone Cypress at Midway Point. (Courtesy of Pat Hathaway.)

FROM ALL THE WORLD THEY COME TO PLAY ✦✦✦ AND PLAY THEY DO

Against this charming Spanish background

GAY rendezvous of travelers to the world's far corners ... society's leaders ... Del Monte's justly famed. Famed for golf beside the ocean and a gorgeous luxury of living.

Here too, you'll find a hundred miles of bridle path ... a smart guest ranch; sport upon a bay as blue as Naples.

And no matter how you crowd the days ... always, you'll find yourself close to the laughing song of an older Spanish life ... serene, yet tuned to the tempo fashionable.

Reservations should be made in advance. Address Carl S. Stanley, Manager.

Hotel
Del Monte
DEL MONTE   CALIFORNIA
Del Monte Lodge   Pebble Beach

This 1930 advertisement for the hotel and lodge reflects the Spanish influence of Monterey's romantic past. A couple rides past the restored mission, and the reader is promised the company of gay travelers and society's leaders amid a luxurious setting. There is also a comparison of Monterey Bay to the blue waters of Naples. (Courtesy of author.)

A new Del Monte train depot was built in the Colonial Revival style of the new hotel. Although the hotel had ceased to enjoy the fulsome support of the Southern Pacific once it was sold to E H. Harriman, people still traveled to Monterey by rail. The Del Monte train continued to rur until 1971. (Courtesy of Pat Hathaway.)

Even though the hotel's stable of fine horses was replaced with a fleet of automobiles in 1907, the traditional horse-drawn "bus" was still used to pick up guests from the depot for years afterward. The ending and beginning of two eras is seen here, with both modes of transport parked in front of the hotel. (Photograph by J. P. Graham; courtesy of Monterey Public Library.)

This 1926 image of the Hotel del Monte at night was sold as a postcard. The white paint gleamed in the dark, and a bevy of cars was clustered between the west sunken garden and the wall that flanked the sun terrace. (Photograph by J. P. Graham; courtesy of Monterey Public Library.)

Morse began publication of *Game and Gossip* in 1926. The quarterly journal chronicled life at the Hotel del Monte and Del Monte Lodge, and exemplified the stylish outdoor culture he envisioned for the Pebble Beach community. Eric Tyrrell-Martin, second from the right, managed the sports aspect of the hotel. This photograph was taken for an article entitled "Is Polo Too Rough?" (Photograph by J. P. Graham; courtesy of Pat Hathaway.)

Polo may have been a rough sport, but it was also an extremely popular one. Here a crowd watche. a match at the Del Monte polo grounds, which were laid out in the center of the racetrack (Courtesy of Pat Hathaway.)

Clark Gable, handsome movie star and amateur sportsman, enjoyed playing polo when he stayed at the Hotel del Monte. He and his wife, actress Carole Lombard, played golf there as well. Some of the scenes from Gable's 1935 movie, *Mutiny on the Bounty*, were filmed in the Monterey harbor. (Photograph by J. P. Graham; courtesy of Pat Hathaway.)

Polo wasn't just for the men. Morse's youngest daughter, Mary, is second from the left. Her mother was Morse's second wife. Three older children from his first marriage lived back East with their mother, but spent summers at Pebble Beach. (Courtesy of Pat Hathaway.)

Actress Ann Harding stands on the balcony of the Del Monte Lodge. (Photograph by J. P. Graham; courtesy of Pat Hathaway.)

Hollywood movie star Joan Bennett and her husband, Gene Markey, honeymooned at the Del Monte Lodge in 1934. (Photograph by J. P. Graham; courtesy of Pat Hathaway.)

Oliver Hardy, one half of the famous Laurel and Hardy team known for their comedy films, sprawls on the Del Monte Golf Course while playing a shot. (Photograph by J. P. Graham; courtesy of Pat Hathaway.)

A foursome plays a hole in front of the clubhouse at the Del Monte course. (Courtesy of Pat Hathaway.)

119

"Barking seals, spouting whales, deer and cormorants" were all a part of the golfing ambience at Pebble Beach. (Courtesy of Pat Hathaway.)

At the age of 22, Charles Seaver hit a ball from the rough beach up over a 100-foot cliff to win the California state amateur championship at Pebble Beach in 1933. (Photograph by J. P. Graham; courtesy of Pat Hathaway.)

Mrs. Overton French, a member of San Francisco's high society, lounges at the Roman Plunge. Behind her are the Misses Harriet and Cornelia Lewthwaite of Portland, Oregon. They stayed at the Hotel del Monte each summer. (Photograph by J. P. Graham; courtesy of Pat Hathaway.)

Members of the polo gallery, from left to right, included Clarence S. Postly, Evelyn Salisbury, Lady Rachel Howard of London, Isabel McCrerry, Mrs. Clarence S. Postly, Mrs. L. McCrerry, and Aiden Roark. Roark was considered an outstanding polo player. (Photograph by J. P. Graham; courtesy of Pat Hathaway.)

William H. Crocker, son of railroad magnate Charles Crocker, plays at the Pebble Beach Golf Links with his daughter, Countess Andre de Limur. Crocker owned a villa in Pebble Beach. Morse tried to borrow money from him when he was attempting to buy the Hotel del Monte but Crocker declined, citing a conflict of interest as he was a principal owner of the property. (Photograph by J. P. Graham; courtesy of Pat Hathaway.)

Marie Dressler, an actress best known for her comedic roles, made her most famous movie, *Tugboat Annie*, in 1933. Here she stands with S. F. B. Morse in front of the clubhouse of the Del Monte course. (Photograph by J. P. Graham; courtesy of Pat Hathaway.)

A tennis match is held on one of the hotel's East Garden courts. Tennis was so popular that matches were also held at Pacific Grove and Salinas. (Photograph by J. P. Graham; courtesy of Pat Hathaway.)

While not as rigorous as golf, polo, or tennis, shooting was another popular sport enjoyed at the Hotel del Monte. The Del Monte Gun Club was built near the racetrack, and it became the headquarters of the Pacific International Trapshooting Association. Many championship meets were held there. (Photograph by J. P. Graham; courtesy of Pat Hathaway.)

Amelia Earhart, shown here walking out of the hotel onto the sun terrace, stayed at the Hotel del Monte shortly before attempting her round-the-world flight from Oakland, California. Her plane disappeared somewhere over the Pacific Ocean in July 1937, on the last leg of her journey. (Courtesy of Naval Postgraduate School.)

A trio of horseback riders lounges in front of the hotel. They may have been planning a ride through the Del Monte Forest, or just ambling around the hotel grounds. (Photograph by J. P. Graham; courtesy of Pat Hathaway.)

ILLUSTRATION CREDITS

ILLUSTRATION CREDITS FOR PAT HATHAWAY'S CALIFORNIA VIEWS

p. 9 #04-57-1
p. 10 #82-45-8
p. 11 #00-24-2
p. 14 #72-8-53
p. 18. #99-23-2
p. 19 #02-5-1
p. 24 #73-127-1
p. 25 #79-7-18 and #97-100-7
p. 26 #79-12-4
p. 27 #96-73-4 and #75-5-2
p. 28 #82-45-2
p. 29 #79-99-1 and #79-99-18
p. 30 #79-99-3
p. 31 #95-11-7 and #94-68-1
p. 32 #89-33-72 and #73-127-2
p. 33 #86-71-1 and #89-93-11
p. 35 #96-53-10 and #77-1-3
p. 36 #74-73-4
p. 37 #83-1-17 and #96-50-14
p. 38 #00-22-1
p. 39 #96-50-35 and #78-10-8
p. 40 #84-93-1 and #96-53-13
p. 42 #97-112-5
p. 43 #89-33-127 and #72-8-132
p. 44 #98-23-5 and #82-48-1
p. 45 #89-3-1
p. 46 #00-77-2 and #70-51-6
p. 47 #77-87-8 and #77-87-10
p. 48 #70-3-1 and #70-51-7
p. 49 #72-48-1 and #97-100-4
p. 50 #72-21-34 and #86-71-21
p. 51 #79-99-26 and #89-33-86
p. 52 #79-99-34 and #79-106-2
p. 53 #02-91-1 and #78-41-1
p. 54 #93-97-2
p. 55 #73-9-1
p. 56–57 #71-1-1
p. 58 #72-17-54
p. 59 #82-3-10
p. 61 #82-45-23 and #96-73-1
p. 62 #73-10-4 and #73-10-3

p. 63 #89-99-1 and #86-71-8
p. 64 #86-71-9 and #97-112-4
p. 65 #91-44-7
p. 66 #76-29-3 and #89-99-5
p. 67 #86-71-3 and #88-6-1
p. 68 #89-99-8
p. 69 #79-18-4 and #96-50-33
p. 70 #73-10-1
p. 71 #96-53-14 and #78-10-1
p. 72 #72-8-29 and #79-106-4
p. 73 #78-7-5 and #72-17-70
p. 75 #72-17-7 and #01-115-1
p. 77 #89-33-249
p. 80 #82-45-5
p. 84 #82-74-1
p. 85 #85-12-9 and #85-12-12
p. 86 #73-28-1 and #73-28-3
p. 87 #77-1-4 and #81-64-1
p. 88 #89-93-8 and #85-4-2
p. 89 #73-2-5 and #80-17-7
p. 90 #82-21-1 and #82-29-10
p. 91 #81-28-1 and #86-63-6
p. 93 #79-41-9 and #83-1-14
p. 94 #83-57-1
p. 95 #91-72-1
p. 96 #80-26-6
p. 97 #85-48-15 and #90-51-39
p. 99 #71-1-121
p. 100–101 #79-96-2 and #79-96-1
p. 102 #86-82-2 and #71-1-135
p. 113 #85-62-1
p. 114 #98-66-14
p. 116 #99-61-13 and #87-46-2
p. 117 #99-61-32 and #80-66-2
p. 118 #99-61-30 and #99-61-36
p. 119 #99-61-38 and #96-85-40
p. 120 #94-86-1 and #99-61-17
p. 121 #99-61-45 and #99-61-5
p. 122 #99-61-41 and #99-61-35
p. 123 #96-43-1 and #82-45-14
p. 124 #99-61-57

BIBLIOGRAPHY

"A California Garden." *Garden and Forest.* 34 (1888).

Aiken, Charles S. "A California Maze." *The Garden Magazine.* 4 (1905).

Arriola, Andrew. *Grounds of the Hotel del Monte.* San Luis Obispo: California Polytechnic State University, 1983.

Barnes, George E. "An Outing: A Few Hours at Monterey and Its Vicinity." *San Francisco Daily Morning Call.* September 3, 1883.

C. W. J. Johnson Collection, California State Library.

Cain, Julie. "Landscaping the Gilded Age: Rudolph Ulrich at Monterey's Hotel del Monte, 1880–1890." *Noticias del Puerto de Monterey* 53 (2004): 3.

Child, Stephen. *Landscape Architecture: A Series of Letters.* Stanford: Stanford University Press, 1927.

Clark, Donald Thomas. *Monterey County Place Names: A Geographical Dictionary.* Carmel Valley, CA: Kestrel Press, 1991.

Collis P. Huntington Papers, California State Library.

"Death of Arthur Brown, Sr." *Architect and Engineer* 49 (April 1917): 1.

Frederick Law Olmsted Papers, Library of Congress Manuscripts Division.

Hotelling, Neal. *Pebble Beach Golf Links: The Official History.* Chelsea, Michigan: Sleeping Bear Press, 1999.

James, G. Wharton. *The HMMBA in California.* Pasadena: G. W. James, 1896.

Lewis, Oscar. *The Big Four: The Story of Huntington, Stanford, Hopkins and Crocker, and of the Building of the Central Pacific.* New York: Alfred A. Knopf, 1938.

Lydon, Sandy. *Chinese Gold: The Chinese in the Monterey Bay Region.* Capitola, CA: Capitola Book Company, 1985.

McGinty, Brian. *The Palace Inns.* Harrisburg, Pennsylvania: Stackpole Books, 1978.

Monterey, California: The Most Charming Summer and Winter Resort in the World, The Most Delightful Sanitarium upon the Pacific Coast, and the Most Equable Temperature in America. Monterey: 1881.

Morrow, William. *Souvenir of the Hotel del Monte*. Del Monte: Hotel del Monte.

Phillips, Morris. *Abroad and At Home: Practical Hints for Tourists*. New York: Art Press, 1891.

Raiquet, William Otis. "Monterey Enchantment," *Architect and Engineer* 87 (October 1926): 1.

Stoddard, Charles Augustus. *Beyond the Rockies: A Spring Journey in California*. New York: C. Scribner's Sons, 1894.

Streatfield, David. *California Gardens: Creating A New Eden*. New York: Abbeville Press, 1994.

Tilman, Jeffrey Thomas. *Arthur Brown Junior, and the Grand Design*. University of Virginia, 1998.

Truman, Benjamin Cummings. *Tourist's Illustrated Guide to the Celebrated Summer and Winter Resorts of California: Adjacent to and upon the Lines of the Central and Southern Pacific Railroads*. San Francisco: H. S. Crocker, 1883.

Vandyke, Paul. "My Studio at Monterey," *Californian Illustrated Magazine* 2 (July 1892): 2.

WPA Guide to the Monterey Peninsula. Tucson: University of Arizona Press, 1989.

Wildman, Rounsevelle. "As Talked in the Sanctum: Del Monte and Monterey." *Overland Monthly* and *Out West* Magazine 26 (December 1895): 156.

Wright, Benjamin Franklin. *Memoirs, Monterey*. Palace Stationery Company, c. 1936.

I've also relied heavily on Hotel del Monte souvenir pamphlets and the *Del Monte Wave*, in addition to numerous items found in the local newspapers published between 1880 and 1942, including the *Monterey Argus*, *Monterey Californian*, *Monterey Cypress*, *Monterey Peninsula Herald*, and the *Salinas Weekly Index*.

The tower of the hotel is reflected amidst the lily pads floating in the circular pool of the west sunken garden. World War II brought an end to the Del Monte as a hotel. Today the Naval Postgraduate School occupies the property. (Photograph by J. P. Graham; courtesy of author.)